The Astronomer Cecilia Payne-Gaposchkin – A Short Biography

By Doug West, Ph.D.

**The Astronomer Cecilia Payne-Gaposchkin –
A Short Biography**

Copyright © 2015 Doug West

All Rights Reserved. No part of this book may be reproduced in any form without written permission from the author. Reviewers may quote brief passages in reviews.

Table of Contents

Preface v

Introduction vii

Chapter 1 - Early Years 1

Chapter 2 – College Years at Cambridge 9

Chapter 3 – Life as a Student at Harvard 15

Chapter 4 – Working at Harvard 21

Chapter 5 – Life in America for the Gaposchkins 25

Chapter 6 – Career Discoveries and Achievements 31

Chapter 7 – Later Life and Recognitions 35

Acknowledgements 39

Further Reading 41

About the Author 43

Index 47

Preface

Welcome to the book *The Astronomer Cecilia Payne-Gaposchkin – A Short Biography*. This book is part of the *30 Minute Book Series* and, as the name of the series implies, if you are an average reader this book will take around 30 minutes to read. Since this book is not meant to be an all-encompassing biography of Cecilia Payne-Gaposchkin, you may want to know more about this accomplished woman. To help you with this, there are several good references at the end of this book. Thank you for purchasing this book and I hope you enjoy your time reading about Cecilia Payne-Gaposchkin.

Doug West

September 2015

Introduction

"Do not undertake a scientific career in quest of fame or money. There are easier and better ways to reach them. Undertake it only if nothing else will satisfy you; for nothing is probably what you will receive. Your reward will be the widening of the horizon as you climb. And if you achieve that reward you will ask no other."

– Cecilia Payne-Gaposchkin

In Cecilia Payne-Gaposchkin's time on this earth, she saw the world change rapidly. She grew up in Victorian England where a lady's place was in the home and there were rigid social rules to be followed if one was to be considered "proper." Her upbringing was little different from that of her ancestors, generations before her. By her adulthood, people were calling family and friends, thanks to the telephone. And they were traveling more; a trip from New York to London took hours rather than days. This connectivity of the world enabled Cecilia to work in conjunction with scientists on other continents. The advances in technology we take for granted now, such as the telephone, radio, television, computer, and automobile, came about during her lifetime. The changes were not only about technology, but also about women, who were moving out of their traditional roles and into the workplace and prominent positions in society.

Doug West, Ph.D.

The life story of Cecilia Payne-Gaposchkin is more than just a story about a woman in science; it is a continuation of the journeys and struggles of women who would not back down. She is a modern example of a woman succeeding through sheer determination and grit. She is unlikely to be put down in the history books as a martyr or a great patron of the women's rights movement, but her contribution to the realm of science and the women's movement should never be understated.

Few people are fortunate enough to be driven by their passions in the way that Cecilia Payne-Gaposchkin was. In fact, most people will never find such a topic that ignites their soul and inspires them every day. It is undoubted that her contributions to the scientific world were monumental. She opened the door for women to be university professors at some of the top schools in the country, made it possible for a woman to be involved in science without scoffs and laughs from male counterparts, and showed us it was possible to balance a career and family. Something to understand about Cecilia Payne-Gaposchkin was that she did not just achieve one goal then sit back and do nothing—every stage of this woman's life, until her very death, was about progressing further and further.

Read on and see her life and work unfold.

CHAPTER 1

Early Years

Cecilia Payne was the first of three children born to Edward John Payne, a London barrister, historian, and Oxford scholar, and Emma Leonora Helena Payne. Cecilia Payne was born May 10, 1900 and brother, Humfry, and her sister, Leonora, followed just a few years later. Their mother was the granddaughter of Parliament member and Hanoverian scholar, Chevalier G.H. Pertz.

Cecilia's father, Edward Payne, was born in 1844 in Buckinghamshire, England, and was well educated with a degree from Oxford University. He read the law and was admitted to the Bar in 1874. Edward was a scholar, and when not practicing law he was writing historical works. He was very musically inclined and was the organist at the High Wycombe Parish Church. Payne was also very active in local affairs, holding the positions of Recorder of High Wycombe and Borough Magistrate.

John and Emma married later in life than most and he was in his mid-fifties by the time Cecilia was born. Though her father passed away at an early age, Cecilia remembers one time when she was upset and he comforted her. It was after the arrival of Humfry's godfather, who came for a visit and offered only Humfry the opportunity to ride in his carriage. Though Cecilia begged to go, she was denied and ran to her father's office upset. Though he was busy writing *History of the New World Called America*, he set aside his pen and told her, "Never mind, Popsy, I'll take you for a walk." As they went on their walk, they ran across the carriage and Edward signaled for it to stop. He hoisted Cecilia up to the driver's bench and she got to ride behind the two horses—a little girl's day had just been made.

The children watched for their father to come home from his office in London each night. He would sit on the floor with the children and build "miniature Stonehenges" out of wooden blocks he had made for them. Cecilia never got the opportunity to get to know her father as well as she wanted, as he died when she was just four years old. According to her own recollection, she remembers the day he died vividly. "I shall say nothing of that traumatic experience, which I remember only too well...For the rest of my childhood, I felt I was not like other children, for I had two fathers in heaven."

While women in Victorian England were not expected, nor encouraged, to be educated, Emma Payne introduced her three children, Cecilia, Humfry, and Leonora, to literature early on in their lives. With the death of her husband, Emma went from being a devoted wife and mother to a single women with three small children under the age of five to support. Emma worked as a painter and musician to make ends meet, and took care of her small children. She was a widow instead of the mother of illegitimate children, which afforded her more societal acceptance than she would have expected otherwise. Emma Payne was able to keep her children in what they needed into adulthood, not only by the selling of her paintings but also by the fact that her family was not impoverished to begin with. Emma also received a small death benefit from the government after the passing of her husband. Money was very tight but Emma managed to keep her family together and raise her young children.

It is lucky for Cecilia and her sister that their mother believed so much in education. Feminists of the time were focused on finding jobs for women and to increase the availability of education to females, but many parents thought it was a waste of time to educate their daughters. During Cecilia's adolescence, she was afforded some of the opportunities which would have been denied to her if she had been born only a few decades earlier.

At age six, Cecilia began her formal education at a small co-educational school close to her home in Wendover. Cecilia was eager to learn to read; in particular, she wanted to read the *Encyclopedia Britannica*. The school had strict rules and emphasized the power of observation and memorization. Cecilia later recalled this training had been very valuable to her as a scientist.

In her autobiography, Cecilia Payne recalls the moment she first felt her heart leap with excitement when she learned about the natural world. „My mother had told me of the Riviera- trapdoor spiders and mimosa and orchids, and I was dazzled by a flash of recognition. For the first time, I knew the leaping of the heart, the sudden enlightenment, that were to become my passion." This is the moment she said that her career as a scientist began. Such was her early love for botany that, while standing in front of a transplanted evergreen, she made a vow to the universe that she would dedicate her life to the study of nature.

When Cecilia was ten years old she saw her first meteor streaking across the sky. Her mother taught Cecilia the rhyme: "As we were walking home that night, we saw a shining meteor." It stuck with Cecilia and she later described her sighting of Halley's Comet as paling in comparison to that first meteor sighting.

Figure – 1783 drawing of a meteor streaking across the sky in England

When Cecilia was around the age of twelve, her mother decided to move the family to London. The primary reason for the move was so that Humfry could get the proper education to prepare him for a good public school. Humfry attended a preparatory school while Cecilia and her sister went to St. Mary's College, Paddington. The school was under the Church of England and religious instruction was emphasized. In her autobiography, Cecilia recounts a nice letter written by one of her teachers when she left the school: "Miss Edwards wrote me a letter of farewell and advice. 'You will always be hampered,' she said, 'by your quick power of apprehension.' She was one of the wisest people I have ever known. I cannot count how often those words have served as a warning against hastily jumping to conclusions."

The time Cecilia Payne spent at St. Mary's School, whose primary focus was on divinity, was not conducive to Cecelia's passion. Her school saw science as being in direct opposition to the divine. The Bible study and church trips left Cecilia hungry for something more. At times, she would fake a fainting spell in order to get out of the trips to church. She was determined to teach science to herself, even if no one would guide her. Fortunately, one of her teachers saw that she was eager to learn and started teaching Cecilia the subjects of botany and chemistry.

The passion which Cecilia had in science was expanding and encompassing all forms of science and math, most particularly botany and algebra. It was here that she was first exposed to the works of Thomas Huxley, Emmanuel Swedenborg, and Sir Isaac Newton. Unlike many of the school age girls who were concerned with who they would wed, Cecilia delighted in pushing her mind to its furthest boundaries.

Due to her Victorian upbringing, Cecilia had little experience with boys. There was a rule in her house that if her brother brought male friends to the house, the girls were expected to not be seen. They had to become scarce to avoid any hint of intrigue. Women of Cecilia's time were expected to find husbands early on, but since her family had little money, it was impressed on her and her sister that this was not a likely possibility for either of them.

Dancing at "coming-out" parties was no treat for Cecilia, though she only attended a few dances in her life. She did not know how to dance and many of her clothes were hand-me-downs from a rich friend's daughter. Once she was embarrassed as the boy she was dancing with recognized the ill-fitting dress and knew it was secondhand. Her conversation skills with young men were not any better than her skills at dancing. While trying to entertain a friend of her brother, she was awkward. The young man would later remark, "Fancy! A girl who reads Plato for pleasure!" The social graces were not young Cecilia's strong suit.

In the next to the last year of her secondary education at St. Mary's, Cecilia was unexpectedly asked to leave the school and transfer to another school. Cecilia was almost 17 years old and she was devastated by the news. This caused her great concern because she knew if she was to go to Cambridge University it would require a scholarship. This dark cloud had a silver lining, as Cecilia would later recall: "Yet if I had but known it, the powers that decided my fate had done me the greatest possible service."

St. Paul's Girls' School was a big improvement for Cecilia over St. Mary's School. St. Paul's was a more modern school and was not church based. The student body was much more diverse; there was a large population of Jewish students and kosher meals were prepared for them. This new school had scientific laboratories and the instructors encouraged her to pursue her dream of becoming a scientist.

The Astronomer Cecilia Payne-Gaposchkin – A Short Biography

Figure – St. Paul's Girls School circa 1907
(photo curtesy St. Paul's Girls School)

Once at St. Paul's, Cecilia had to begin preparation for competitive scholarships to Cambridge University. The instructor that was of great help to her was Miss Ivy Pendleburg. She led Cecilia through a study of mechanics and rigid dynamics, electricity and magnetics, light and thermodynamics, and a bit of astronomy. By this time, physics had replaced botany as Cecilia's topic of interest. This preparation for the university paid off handsomely as Cecilia received a scholarship to Newnham College, a Cambridge University affiliate.

CHAPTER 2

College Years at Cambridge

When Cecilia first received her scholarship to Newnham College in 1919, she was excited about the possibilities this new opportunity provided for her. She was still unsure of which scientific field she should pursue, so Cecilia focused on the natural sciences, specifically botany. Her specific areas of focus expanded later to include chemistry, botany, and physics, with her primary focus being on the latter. It was a strange combination for a natural science student, but Cecilia insisted.

The study of botany, more specifically paleo-botany, did not excite her as much as she had hoped. From the start, she had trouble affording textbooks. The lectures given on botany covered topics with which Cecilia was already familiar, so they provided her with little stimulation. Once, her passion was briefly reignited when she was examining a rather mediocre form of algae. She found a group of desmids through the microscope and asked her instructor to help her identify them. Instead of feeding her thirst for knowledge, her professor said, "They don't come into your course," and left it at that. Even trying to engage her professors in deeper conversation on the subject of paleo-botany left Cecilia without fulfillment as they offered her "neither inspiration not encouragement."

After a year studying the natural sciences, Cecilia attended a lecture given by Arthur Eddington, Cambridge College's foremost expert on astronomy. Eddington was noted for his expedition to the Island of Principle to observe a total solar eclipse, and the implications of the discoveries he made there on Einstein's theory of relativity. She was so taken by Eddington's words that she transcribed his speech verbatim that evening. She later wrote about her experience right after the lecture. "For three nights, I think, I did not sleep. My world had been so shaken that I experienced something like a nervous breakdown. The experience was so acute, so personal..." It was from this moment that she resolved to become an astronomer. Eddington saw something in her which inspired him to take the young Cecilia Payne under his wing.

Figure – Total Solar Eclipse photograph taken by Arthur Eddington in 1919

The Astronomer Cecilia Payne-Gaposchkin – A Short Biography

An issue became apparent that would affect her dream, which was that she was too far into her studies of botany to be allowed to change her major to astronomy, as it was part of the mathematics department. Though this was a saddening reality for Payne, it did little to deter her. She kept studying the natural sciences and took all of the lectures and classes on astronomy that she could fit into her schedule. She also presided over the Newnham College Astronomical Society, which allowed her to exchange ideas with others interested in astronomy.

One of her professors was the physicist Ernest Rutherford, who was teaching and conducting research at the Cavendish Laboratory. Rutherford harassed Cecilia a great deal since she was the only female student in the class. Her classmates were not supportive either. Rutherford frequently tried to get the men in the class to laugh at her, especially since women were required to sit in the front row away from the males. This type of treatment was common, so she had to develop a thick skin early on.

Her laboratory work was difficult and Cecilia knew that she needed a tutor. Newnham College provided no tutors for physics so Cecilia was passed from tutor to tutor. Because of her shyness and inexperience with men, she was afraid to ask questions and made many mistakes along the way. She remarked later that she learned very little about experimental physics during her time at Cambridge.

One of her better experiences while at Cambridge was her new friendship with L.J. Comrie, a World War I veteran from Australia working on an advanced degree at Cambridge. The Observatory at Newnham College had been largely in a state of disrepair. With the aid of Comrie, Payne was able to get the observatory back into working order.

During a visit to the Solar Physics Observatory, she met astronomer Edward Milne, who was second in command of the observatory. They became and remained close friends over the years. She had other friends at college, mostly female art majors whom she tried to pull into her excitement for astronomy. Though she later remarked that much of the theories were lost on them, they frequently listened. One of her friends later said that Payne despised chairs, but when she lay on her back in bed she would discuss anything from ethics to making cocoa.

It was at the advice of one of her closest friends, Comrie, that Payne first considered moving to America. Comrie had suggested that, as a woman, she would have more opportunities provided to her in the United States than she would in England. In 1922, Comrie escorted Cecilia to the centennial meeting of the Royal Astronomical Society, and it was here that they first heard a lecture given by Harlow Shapley of the Harvard College Observatory. The passion of his words made Payne more determined than ever to move to the United States and work for Harvard College Observatory. She soon realized that the only career which would be available to her if she stayed in England was that of a teacher. Though Cecilia had once had the ambition of being a teacher, this had changed with time, education, and exposure to a world beyond the confines of England.

The Astronomer Cecilia Payne-Gaposchkin – A Short Biography

Figure – Harlow Shapley

Cecilia completed her coursework in 1923 at Newnham College, Cambridge University. This was a great success, but at the time women were not allowed to receive formal degrees in England, so despite her education and good grades, Cecilia Payne did not have the paperwork to back up her hard work.

To achieve an advanced degree in England and to continue her work was not likely. After meeting Dr. Shapley, she applied for a Pickering Fellowship through Harvard College; the award was reserved exclusively to women. She received the scholarship and had enough money to move to the United States and study for a year at Harvard. She ended up spending her whole career in Boston, Massachusetts, a place she lovingly called her "stony-hearted stepmother." She was the second woman to receive this fellowship through Harvard, the first being Adelaide James.

CHAPTER 3

Life as a Student at Harvard

Harlow Shapley might have been worried about hiring Payne since her major was neither in astronomy nor math, had it not been for the amazing recommendations given by Eddington and Comrie. Comrie commented that she was likely the type to devote her whole life to the field and not run off to get married after a few years. The worry that a woman would abandon her career to get married and have children was a concern voiced by many employers and used as a reason to not hire women for most jobs. While Cecilia did eventually get married, she also devoted the whole of her adult life to astronomy. Cecilia's dedication to her love of astronomy can be seen by how willingly she packed up her belongings and left everything and everyone she knew to form a new life in the United States. This was not something a lot of women did in the 1920s. There were some now famous women traveling at the time, but the majority of women were just beginning to flex their wings of independence.

When Cecilia began working at Harvard College Observatory, she was under the direct guidance of Harlow Shapley, who was already a prominent astronomer and had built his reputation on his work with eclipsing binary stars and his measurements of the size of the galaxy. Harlow Shapley was a young and ambitious astronomer and director of the Harvard

College Observatory. His plan was to grow the staff of the observatory and raise the prominence of the observatory in the world of astronomy. To achieve his goals for the observatory, he needed top people and at that time there was a shortage of astronomers. Few institutions of higher education produced Ph.D. level astronomers, and they were in short supply. In the early 20th century, the science of astronomy was evolving from nearly a purely observational science to the new science of astrophysics. Astrophysics was combining the knowledge from the areas of physics, chemistry, and mathematics to explain the systems of stars and planets that astronomers were observing. Cecilia Payne's formal education in physics and astronomy had prepared her to become a player in this emerging new science.

Life in the United States was different than Cecilia was used to in England. The common view the British held of Americans at the time was that they were all "wealthy and poorly-educated." Cecilia found herself on more than one occasion explaining to her family that this was simply not true. One time specifically, Cecilia bought a car. The use of cars became a necessity in America before they did in England, and Cecilia's family saw this "necessity" as a sign of wealth and frivolity.

One of the greatest differences that Cecilia remarked upon between the two countries was in the education system. While her education was regulated by gender and social class, the United States had children going to public schools where children of each gender and every social class intermingled. While she is glad for the upbringing she had, Cecilia marveled that American children were encouraged early on to become individuals and develop their own ideas.

The Astronomer Cecilia Payne-Gaposchkin – A Short Biography

As a young woman, Cecilia adored and admired Harlow Shapley. He was very active in what every staff member was doing, and he offered encouragement, even to the women. This was something she had received little of from men before. Cecilia was not a regular employee like the other women working at Harvard College Observatory; she was on a fellowship and as such had the choice of which area she wanted to focus her research on. Shapley had hoped that Payne would carry on the photometric work of Miss Leavitt, but Cecilia was determined to follow a path of her own. In her last year at Cambridge, Cecilia became familiar with the work of Indian physicist Meghnad Saha. Saha's idea of merging physical chemistry and the ionization of stellar material eventually led to the development of the field of astrophysics. When Cecilia told Shapley that this was her intended path of study, he quickly made all of the photographic plates available to her. Harvard College Observatory had been routinely photographing the sky since the 1880s and probably had the world's most extensive collection of photographic plates of the night sky.

It was during her classes at Radcliffe College, a division of Harvard, that Cecilia worked on her doctorate, which was an opportunity she would not have had if she had stayed in England. In Cecilia's thesis, entitled *Stellar Atmospheres*, she proposed a composition of stars which was based on the theory of the abundance of helium and hydrogen in the universe. Cecilia was the first person to propose that the simplest element, hydrogen, was actually the most abundant element in the universe. She suggested that the range in strength between stars and the absorption lines of the stellar spectra were due to different temperatures and not on a varying chemical composition, as previously thought. Her thesis expounded on the work of Saha, which theorized that there was a correlation between ionization of stars to their temperature and chemical density. Cecilia was able to apply the ionization formula developed by Saha to relate the spectral classes of stars to their actual temperature. Instead of attributing stellar absorption lines to different combinations of elements, Cecilia theorized that stars had the same basic chemical composition and attributed the difference in their colors on the temperature difference.

Figure – Harvard College Observatory circa 1899

The common belief among astronomers at the time was that the presence of silicon, carbon, and other elements on earth was the same composition which could be found in stars, and in the same relevant amounts. This theory had evidence in the analysis of the sun's spectra, which showed these elements. Payne did find this assessment to be correct, at least as it pertains to the Earth. The exciting and at times controversial assessment she made was that hydrogen and helium, being the most common elements in the universe, must be the primary components of stars. Hydrogen was the far greater element in terms of abundance, being more prevalent than helium by about one million times. When Payne published her work, astronomers Otto Struve and Velta Zebergs referred to it as "undoubtedly the most brilliant Ph.D. thesis ever written."

There was a bit of regret in Cecilia's undertaking of her thesis. She recounts one day being called into the office of Harlow Shapley. He looked rueful as he told her that Henry Russell Norris was sending his student, Donald Menzel, down to look at the same photographic plates she was using. Norris and Menzel had also seen the potential in Saha's theory and had planned to work on a thesis similar to hers. The regret came from Cecilia in not seeing the collaborative opportunity between Menzel and herself. Menzel had been trained in the use of spectrographic equipment and techniques, which was an opportunity which Cecilia had not been afforded.

Though Cecilia's conclusion on the composition of the stars has since become the basis for the analysis of the cosmos, she was at the time persuaded to write a less definitive statement by her male superiors, particularly Henry Norris Russell. He was unnerved by the fact that her thesis contradicted the prevalent model of the universe. Years later, Norris came to the same conclusion and when he later published his book of stellar spectra he credited Cecilia Payne with her discovery.

She received her Ph.D. from Radcliffe College. After graduation, she continued at Harvard on a post-doctoral fellowship.

Before her fellowship ended, Shapley offered Cecilia a paid staff position, and she accepted the offer at a salary of $2,100 a year.

CHAPTER 4

Working at Harvard

It was in 1928 that Payne's thesis work on the composition of stars was finally published by Harvard. It was the first research of its kind and truly groundbreaking in the field of astronomy, though, as new ideas often do, it initially met with some resistance from the scientific community. The resistance waned as Payne discovered more evidence to support her theory through the analysis of stellar spectra to determine their composition and temperature.

During Cecilia's early career at Harvard, she was under the shadow of the lead female astronomer, Annie Jump Cannon. Ms. Cannon belonged to a generation in which men supervised, while women cataloged. Cecilia belonged to a time when women were just beginning to challenge gender roles and work independently. Her compilation was small in comparison to that of Annie Jump Cannon, who had compiled thousands of stellar spectra in nine volumes of the Henry Draper Catalog.

Figure – Annie J. Cannon (Courtesy AAVSO)

Cecilia Payne fulfilled her dream and became a full American citizen in 1931, and another major life event occurred for her in 1933, when she met her future husband while visiting Germany. The following year she married the Russian astrophysicists, Sergei Gaposchkin, thus helping him gain American citizenship as well. She collaborated with him on much of her research throughout her career. It was with her husband that she identified and measured many variable stars on photographic plates.

Payne-Gaposchkin was known for her phenomenal memory, which made her a walking wealth of scientific knowledge. With the aid of her husband, she moved into the field of variable stars and did research on the composition and structure of the Milky Way Galaxy. The wealth of their studies came from the two million star magnitudes which they measured within the Magellanic Clouds.

Figure – Female astronomy staff at Harvard College Observatory. Cecilia is in the center of the top row.
(Courtesy AAVSO)

Before Payne-Gaposchkin received the formal title of Professor at Harvard, she still participated in many of the roles a professor was expected to, despite her actual title being "technical assistant" to Professor Shapley. At this time, she made a mere $2,300 per year but did not let this dissuade her from the obligations of a partial professor. She still gave lectures at the University, performed research, and advised students. In 1938 she became the Phillips Astronomer of the Harvard College Observatory. With the help of Donald Menzel, in 1956, she became the first female full professor at Harvard and was granted the role of Astronomy Department Chair, the first female chair at Harvard. For her new position and responsibilities, her salary rose to $10,000 per year. This was still below the range of $12,000 to $14,000 a professor would make at a similar university. She watched many times as male junior associate professor would come into the department at a lower salary and pass her by within a few years. By the time she retired in 1966, her salary had risen to $15,000, which was an improvement but unfortunately, it was less than every other member of the faculty, except for one female that was twenty years her junior. The lower pay scale for females was something Cecilia never liked, but had learned to live with.

CHAPTER 5

Life in America for the Gaposchkins

Cecilia traveled to Göttingen, Germany in 1933 for the meeting of the Astronomische Gesellschaft. Though everyone was kind, Payne did not know most of the astronomers at the conference. She recalls sitting shyly at one of the tables and having someone bring her mail into her. It was a man who addressed her and asked, „Sind Sie, Miss Payne?" She told him she was. This man, named Sergei Gaposchkin, was surprised by how young she was and he had expected Miss Payne to be a little old lady. Sergei had prepared a short biography of himself, which told of his plight as an exile to find a safe country in which to live and work. Due to his politics, he could not return to Russia and the tensions between Germany and Russia prevented him from staying long term in Germany. The story touched Cecilia's heart because he had struggled to follow his dreams, just as she had. She later admitted that there were not many sleepless nights in her life, but as she lay in bed concerned for Sergei's well-being and determined to help him start a new life, she slept not a wink that night.

Sergei was living in political exile in Germany at the time. He was born in July of 1889, the son of a day laborer and one of 11 children. After completing elementary school, Sergei moved to Moscow and began working in a textile factory. He was there for two years before being called to military service in the Tsar's army. After his military service was complete, Sergei served as a police officer in his hometown. He attended classes at night to complete his education.

By the time Cecilia and Sergei met, he was not allowed to return to Russia because of his political views. Cecilia used her connections to secure a position for Sergei at Harvard College. The couple dated quietly and, in March of 1934, their passion for each other led them to be wed. They were not only partners in life, but also partners in astronomy. Cecilia and Sergei's wedding turned out to a surprise for nearly everyone at the observatory. They had kept their blossoming relationship quiet until they were married. Most felt the coarse Russian and the refined English astronomer were a mismatch—time would prove them very wrong.

Cecilia and Sergei had three children together. Their eldest, Edward, was born in 1935. Two years later, Katherine joined the family, and in 1940, their family was complete with the birth of Peter. The youngest son, Peter, became a physicist and a programming analyst, following closely to his parents line of work. Katherine went on to write the full biography of her mother.

Cecilia did not see the world of religion as conflicting with science, rather both as embracing each other. One of Cecilia Payne-Gaposchkin's side projects was to teach Sunday School. Every Sunday she would head over to the Unitarian Church in Lexington, which was three miles away, and teach a group of nine to twelve-year-olds. It is perhaps for the best that Cecilia was not drawn to dedicate her life solely to the church, but instead to science. She said, "If my religious passion had turned toward the Catholic Church I should have wanted to be a priest. I am sure that I would have never settled for being a nun." She had dreams that were big and, despite opposition, she did what needed to be done. This meant a great deal to her daughter and biographer, Katherine Haramundanis, who recounted one particularly cold Sunday morning when the car would not start. This did not stop her from going to Church; instead, she put on heavy wool slacks and walked over three miles in the snow. Just as with other aspects of her life, Cecilia kept going, taking one step at a time, not deterred by snow, slow promotions, or low pay. Cecilia herself said, "I simply went on plodding, rewarded by the beauty of the scenery, towards an unexpected goal." This was the type of character she had. When she wasn't teaching Sunday school, researching the night sky, or being a wife and devoted mother, Cecilia kept herself busy with needlepoint. She was also an avid knitter and loved to read detective novels.

The 1930s brought with them dramatic changes in the United States and much of the world entering into the Great Depression. It would take World War II to force America out of its economic malaise. While much of the United States was swept into turmoil at this time, Cecilia and her husband were not affected as much as many others. It was not always easy for the two, especially early on in their marriage. Money was tight and either she or Sergei would have to stay home with the children while the other attended some conference or lecture.

In July of 1939, the Gaposchkins took their children to Paris for the conference on Novae and White Dwarf stars. At the time, no one suspected the strong link these two bodies would have on each other. They went to dinner and had a riveting conversation with Sir Arthur Eddington and Frederic Joliot. Joliot sparked Cecilia's imagination with the research he was doing on chain reactions in the universe. This was the last time Cecilia would see her mentor Eddington, as he died from cancer in 1944.

After they left France, the Gaposchkins headed to England so their children could meet family members. She regaled them with stories from her youth and engaged in games at her childhood home. After the visit they boarded the French liner *Normandie* at Southhampton, and the ship began the long journey to New York on the evening of August 23. War tensions filled the air on board and the ship's captain ordered the speed increased and the radio operators to cease all transmission. As more news of the pending war in Europe reached the ship, the captain adopted a zigzag course to evade possible torpedoes and all cabin curtains were to be drawn at night to effectively "black out" the ship to avoid possible encounters with hostile German ships or submarines. The *Normandie* arrived safely in New York on August 28, just three days before Hitler invaded Poland. With both of their families being an ocean closer to the war, it was a troubled time for the Gaposchkin family.

As a response to the war, around 1940 the Gaposchkins purchased a small farm in the nearby town of Townsend. They wanted to contribute to the food supply, for themselves and others, as well as provide employment for refugee families. Since nearly all the refugees they knew were academics, they didn't find any families interested in farm work. The Gaposchkins did much of the work themselves and relied on some of their neighbors in Townsend for help. On the farm, they had a cow, a sheep, and poultry. Sergei loved the farm much more than Cecilia did. On Sundays, they would deliver as many as one thousand eggs to the local market for sale.

During the war years, Cecilia and Sergei hosted weekly meetings of the Forum for International Problems, to educate those who attended on the background and history of Italy, Spain, Russia, Israel, and more. Shapley supported this endeavor and offered the observatory as a place to hold the meetings. They believed that people in the United States did not know enough about what was going on in the world. Every week these presentations turned into debates.

Cecilia had long held a passion for traveling, which she probably inherited from her mother, who also enjoyed traveling. Some of the places Cecilia ventured to over the years were her home country of England, as well as Germany, Austria, Mexico, Canada, Russia, Trinidad and Tobago, Italy, and more.

CHAPTER 6

Career Discoveries and Achievements

The work Cecilia Payne-Gaposchkin is most known for is her thesis, *Stellar Atmospheres*, which was where she originally posed that hydrogen was the most abundant of all the elements. This work is still cited by hundreds of astronomy students every year and it is as valid today as it was when it was written. Her thesis was later made into a book, which was well received by other astronomers. Though her thesis initially met with resistance, a few years after publishing her book of the same title, it was clear to astronomers all over the world that Cecilia was indeed correct in her assessment. With the aid of her colleagues, a method of determining a star's temperature was devised based on the visible spectra.

Much of the work Payne-Gaposchkin did after her marriage to Sergei was on understanding variable stars. She sought to understand why these variable stars changed brightness, and why some change for a fraction of a second and others require years to complete a cycle of light variation. An emphasis area of her work, especially later in life, focused on galactic novae. In her memoirs, Payne-Gaposchkin remarks that out of all of her accomplishments, the discovery she made of T Pyx was among her favorites. T Pyx was the first identified recurrent novae, which is a type of star that can remain dim for a decade and then increase in brightness a hundred-fold within hours then slowly fade back into a dim state over the next few months.

With all the firsts she had in her life, T Pyx may be at the top, but other moments also brought her a great deal of pleasure, as she wrote: "My first sight of the spectrum Gamma Velorum, the realization that planetary nebulae are expanding and not rotating, the fact that U Gruis and RY Scuti are eclipsing stars, the true nature of T Ceti, the period of AE Aquarii, the bright-line nature of the supernova spectrum, these are some of the moments of ecstasy that I treasure in retrospect."

Cecilia's expertise in variable stars was widely recognized. Fred Whipple would later write on her knowledge: "Unbelievably detailed knowledge about variable stars is a source of wonder and a source of vital information to astronomers everywhere." Researchers would travel to Harvard just to meet with Cecilia and Sergei to discuss variable stars.

Cecilia was a prolific writer and editor, and her publications span six decades. Her first publication came in 1923, under the guidance of Arthur Eddington, on the proper motion of the stars in the neighborhood of M36. During her lifetime, Cecilia Payne-Gaposchkin wrote many academic books and papers in her field. Her thesis, as previously stated, was made into a book called *Stellar Atmospheres* and was published in 1925 by Radcliffe College. Her next book, *The Stars of High Luminosity,* was published in 1930 and delves into dwarf and giant stars and how they are different from highly luminous stars in their structure.

The Astronomer Cecilia Payne-Gaposchkin – A Short Biography

Cecilia co-authored the book, *Variable Stars,* with her husband in 1938 and it was noted by the *Harvard Review* to be a trailblazing work. Her next two books, *Variable Stars and Galactic Structure* and *The Galactic Novae*, further expounded on her research into the stars. They were published in 1954 and 1957, respectively. The book, *The Galactic Novae,* has been one of her works most cited by other astronomers. She also wrote about the behavior, development, and "birth process" of stars in *Stars in the Making* in 1952, and *Stars and Cluster* in 1979.

CHAPTER 7

Later Life and Recognitions

In the 1950s, Cecilia began to develop a stronger interest in her heritage. When one of Cecilia's aunts died and left her a trunk full of fragile papers and dusty documents, Cecilia took on the task of sorting and reviewing them. The task was not as easily said as done, for much of the correspondence had no names and no dates; a large portion of it was faded, written in several languages, and a few even had crossed writing. These hundreds of documents became the basis for a privately published book, *The Garnett Letters*, which Cecilia finally published at the age of 79.

After over four decades of service, Cecilia Payne-Gaposchkin officially retired from Harvard in 1966. After retirement, she stayed active in the work of the observatory, since renamed the Smithsonian Astrophysical Observatory, and continued to teach some classes at Harvard until 1976.

Despite her being one of the most brilliant and creative 20th century astronomers, and despite her recognition at Harvard, Payne-Gaposchkin was never elected to the elite National Academy of Sciences. She did receive many other honors in her lifetime, especially towards the end of it. The first award she received for her scientific contributions came when she was elected as a member of the Royal Astronomical Society in 1923, while she was at Cambridge. The National Research Council Fellowship from Harvard Observatory, which ultimately led to her moving to the United States, was received the following year. This is the same year in which she became a member of the American Astronomical Society.

Both the American Philosophical Society and the Academy of Arts and Sciences made her an official member in 1936 and 1943, respectively. These memberships were uncommon for women during Payne-Gaposchkin's time. The American Astronomical Society recognized her contributions to her field and awarded her the Annie J. Cannon Prize in 1934. Two years later, she became a member of the American Philosophical Society. This was the beginning of a long line of awards, recognitions, and honorary doctorates she would receive. Her honorary doctorates came from Wilson College in 1942, Smith College in 1943, Western College in 1951, Colby College in 1958, and Women's Medical College of Philadelphia in 1961. She also received a Master of Arts and Doctorate in Science from Cambridge. Radcliffe College gave her an award of Merit and the Franklin Institute presented her with the Rittenhouse Medal. In 1977, the minor planet 1974 CA was officially renamed "Payne-Gaposchkin" in her honor.

The Henry Norris Russell Prize from the American Astronomical Society was presented to her in 1976 to "commemorate a lifetime of pre-eminence in astronomical research and, as such, is awarded to senior astronomers." During her recipient speech, Payne-Gaposchkin said, "The reward of the young scientist is the emotional thrill of being the first person in the history of the world to see something or to understand something. Nothing can compare with that experience...The reward of the old scientist is the sense of having seen a vague sketch grow into a masterly landscape." She, as much as any other astronomer, understood the lifetime of dedication needed to appreciate this high honor.

Cecilia became ill and spent the last few weeks of her life in the hospital. Her old friend Frances Wright visited her in the hospital and found her weakened and confused. Cecilia died on December 7, 1979. The "botanist of the stars" had passed from this life into the next. At her memorial service at Lexington Church, music was played on the organ that she had donated to the church. This was the same organ that her father had played for her when she was a child.

After her passing, she was eulogized with great respect and admiration by many of her old friends and fellow astronomers. According to California Institute of Technology professor, J. Greenstein, she was "charming and humorous." Her daughter Katherine remembers her as "...an inspired seamstress, an inventive knitter, and a voracious reader." When she left the earthly realm, the scientific community was both saddened for losing her and grateful that they had gotten to know her and that she had the opportunity to make so many progressive steps in the world of astronomy.

After Cecilia's death, Sergei was lost and became depressed and gloomy. Cecilia had been at the center of his world for over forty years and it would take time for him to heal the emptiness he felt. Sergei remained living alone in their house in Lexington. He was terribly lonely and started attending the Episcopal Church in Lexington; there he found friendly faces and enjoyed the social activities at the church. Over time, his energy for life returned and he enjoyed his old activities of swimming, biking, and even visiting the observatory occasionally. His health began to decline gradually and after an apparent stoke, he was placed in a nursing home and then a hospital. He had lost his power of speech but enjoyed having friends and family visit him in the hospital. His body gave in to the inevitable, and Sergei died on October 17, 1984.

Acknowledgments

I would like to thank the following individuals for their contributions to this book: Ashley Collins, Lisa Zahn, and Howard Bailes of the St. Paul's Girls School in London for background information and pictures. I would like to also thank The American Association of Variable Star Observers (AAVSO) for pictures.

Further Reading

Boyd, Sylvia L., *Portrait of a Binary – The Lives of Cecilia Payne and Sergei Gaposchkin*. Penobscot Press. 2014.

Haramundanis, Katherine, editor, *Cecilia Payne-Gaposchkin.* Cambridge University Press.1984, 1996.

Hilhorn, H. Thomas. *The History of Astronomy and Astrophysics: A Biographical Approach.* VBW Publishing. 2008.

Douglas, A. Vibert. *Encyclopedia Britannica.* Sir Arthur Stanley Eddington.

West, Doug. *Harlow Shapley - Biography of an Astronomer: The Man Who Measured the Universe.* C&D Publishing. 2015.

About the Author

Doug West is a retired engineer, small business owner, and experienced non-fiction writer with several books to his credit. His writing interests are general, with expertise in science, history, biographies, numismatics, and "How to" topics. Doug has a B.S. in Physics from the Missouri School of Science and Technology and a Ph.D. in General Engineering from Oklahoma State University. He lives with his wife and little dog, "Scrappy," near Kansas City, Missouri. Additional books by Doug West can be found at http://www.amazon.com/Doug-West/e/B00961PJ8M. Follow the author on Facebook at: https://www.facebook.com/30minutebooks.

Figure – Doug West

Additional Books in the "30 Minute Book Series"

A Short Biography of the Scientist Sir Isaac Newton

A Short Biography of the Astronomer Edwin Hubble

Galileo Galilei – A Short Biography

Benjamin Franklin – A Short Biography

The American Revolutionary War – A Short History

Index

A

Astrophysics 16, 41

C

Cambridge University 6, 7, 13, 41
Cannon, Annie 21, 22, 36
Church 1, 4, 26, 37

E

Eddington, Arthur 9, 10, 28, 32
England vii, 1, 2, 4, 12, 13, 16, 17, 28, 29

G

Gaposchkin, Sergei 22, 25, 41

H

Harvard College Observatory 12, 15, 17, 18, 23, 24
Huxley, Thomas 5

L

Leavitt, H. 17
London vii, 1, 2, 4, 39

M

Magellanic Clouds 23
Menzel, Donald 19, 24
meteor 4
Milne, Edward 12

N

Newnham College 7, 9, 11, 13
Novae 27, 33

O

Oxford University 1

P

Payne, Edward 1
Payne, Emma 2
Payne-Gaposchkin, Cecilia i, ii, v, vii, viii, 22, 23, 26, 31, 32, 35, 36, 41

R

Radcliffe College 17, 20, 32, 36
Russell, Henry Norris 19, 36
Rutherford, Ernest 11

S

Saha, Meghnad 17
Shapley, Harlow 12, 13, 15, 17, 19, 41
Stellar Atmospheres 17, 31, 32
St. Mary's School 5, 6
Swedenborg, Emmanuel 5

T

T Pyx 31, 32

U

United States 12, 14, 15, 16, 27, 29, 36

V

variable stars 22, 31, 32

Printed in Great Britain
by Amazon